The Life and Work of...

Joseph Turner

Jayne Woodhouse

Heinemann Library
Chicago, Illinois

© 2001 Reed Educational & Professional Publishing
Published by Heinemann Library,
an imprint of Reed Educational & Professional Publishing,
100 N. LaSalle, Suite 1010
Chicago, IL 60602
Customer Service 888-454-2279
Visit our website at www.heinemannlibrary.com

Designed by Celia Floyd
Illustrations by Sally Barton
Originated by Dot Gradations
Printed in Hong Kong/China

05 04 03 02
10 9 8 7 6 5 4 3 2
Library of Congress Cataloging-in-Publication Data
Woodhouse, Jayne, 1952-
      Joseph Turner / Jayne Woodhouse.
         p. cm. – (The Life and work of--)
      Includes bibliographical references and index.
      Summary: An introduction to the life and work of the nineteenth-century English painter, Joseph Turner, describing the development of his techniques and showing some of his different paintings.
      ISBN 1-57572-345-X
      1. Turner, J. M. W. (Joseph Mallord William), 1775-1851—Juvenile literature. 2. Painters—England—Biography—Juvenile literature. [1. Turner, J. M. W. (Joseph Mallord William), 1775-1851. 2. Artists.] I. Title. II. Series.
ND497.T8 W58 2000
759.2—dc21

[B]   00-025784

Acknowledgments
The author and publishers are grateful to the following for permission to reproduce copyright material: Ashmolean Museum, Oxford, p. 7; Bridgeman Art Library/National Gallery, London, pp. 5, 9; Reading University, Berkshire, p. 24; Agnew & Sons, London, p. 27; E.T. Archive, p. 4; Indianapolis Museum of Art, gift in memory of Dr. and Mrs. Hugo O. Pantzer, p. 11; Robert Harding Picture Library/Ellen Rooney, pp. 18, 20, 26, 28; Tate Picture Library, pp. 19, 21, 23, 25, 29; The Whitworth Art Gallery, p. 15; Yale Center for British Art/Paul Mellon Collection, p. 12

Cover photograph reproduced with permission of The Bridgeman Art Library

Some words are shown in bold, **like this.** You can find out what they mean by looking in the glossary.

Contents

Who Was Joseph Turner?

Joseph Mallord William Turner was a great **landscape** artist. His work changed the way people thought about landscape painting.

Joseph is often called "the painter of light."
This is because of the special way he showed the
changing sky and weather in his paintings.

Early Years

Joseph was born in this house in London, England. It was April 23, 1775, more than 200 years ago. His father was a barber. His mother was unwell for much of her life.

Joseph started drawing as a young boy. His father was proud of his pictures and hung them in his barbershop. Joseph drew this picture when he was twelve years old.

A Love of the Sea

When he was young, Joseph loved to watch the ships sail. One day he saw a picture of a ship at sea. It made him want to be a painter.

All his life, Joseph painted ships and the sea. In 1838, when he was 63, he painted this picture. It is a famous fighting ship on its last journey.

Learning to Be an Artist

When he was fourteen, Joseph began studying art. He went to the **Royal Academy** in London. He drew pictures of **statues**. The statues were from **ancient** Greece and Rome.

A year later, in 1790, Joseph **exhibited** his first painting at the Royal Academy. He was only fifteen years old. It was already clear that he was very talented.

The Royal Academy

Joseph **exhibited** his paintings at the **Royal Academy** all his life. This picture shows people visiting the **gallery** in Joseph's time. Look how close together the paintings are placed.

When Joseph was 32, he became a **professor** at the Royal Academy. He made many careful drawings like this one. He used his drawings to teach students about painting and drawing.

Travels in England

At the age of seventeen, Joseph took the first of his many travels. He was always looking for something new to draw and paint.

At first, Joseph visited places in England. His first paintings were **watercolors** of the things he saw. Joseph painted Canterbury **Cathedral** in 1794. He was nineteen.

Travels in Europe

In his lifetime, Joseph traveled to many places. Traveling was much slower and harder then. There were no cars or planes. Joseph often walked many miles in a day.

Joseph made **sketches** of what he saw. Later, he turned his sketches into finished paintings. Here is his painting of the German countryside. He painted it three years after his visit there.

Old Masters

In 1802, Joseph visited the **Louvre** Museum in Paris, France. He studied the Louvre's famous collection of **old masters**. This is a photograph of the Louvre today.

Joseph liked the paintings of the old masters. He tried different ideas as he painted with **oils**. This painting is in the same **style** as a great French painter named Poussin.

A Visitor at Petworth

Joseph's work was admired by many people. One collector of Joseph's paintings owned a great country house in England. The house was named Petworth House. Here is Petworth House today.

From the age of 34, Joseph often visited Petworth House. He had his own **studio** there. He made many **sketches** and paintings of the house and its huge **grounds**.

Sketches

Joseph liked to paint things he had seen himself. In 1810, he was staying in a town in northern England. A terrible storm came up. Joseph quickly made **sketches** of it on the back of a letter.

Two years later, he used those sketches to help make this painting. You can see the storm sweeping across the mountains.

Ways of Working

Joseph often worked in unusual ways. Sometimes he finished his pictures while they hung on the **gallery** walls. He was still painting the day before the **exhibition** opened!

This painting shows a ship caught in a snow storm. There is a story that Joseph was on this ship that day. The story said that Joseph asked the sailors to tie him to the **mast.** He wanted to see what the storm was really like.

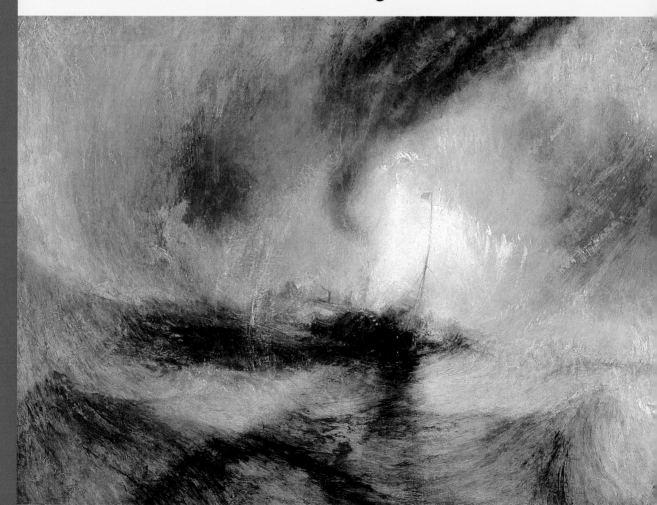

New Directions

An important change in Joseph's work came on his first visit to Venice, Italy, in 1819. The dazzling Italian light gave him new ideas about how to show shape and color.

Joseph returned to Venice several times. He painted many pictures of its famous buildings and waterways. He finished this one in 1840, when he was 65 years old.

Joseph Dies

Joseph painted almost to the end of his life. He died in 1851, at the age of 76. He was buried in St Paul's **Cathedral** in London, England.

Many of his later paintings were **abstract**. They were full of swirling light. People didn't like these paintings. They called them "pictures of nothing." Now people call them **masterpieces**.

Timeline

1775	Joseph Turner born in London on April 23
1789	Starts studying art at the **Royal Academy**
1790	First painting **exhibited**
1792	First **sketching** tour in England and Wales
1802	First tour of France and Switzerland
1804	Opens own **gallery**
1807	Becomes **professor** at Royal Academy
1809	First visit to Petworth House
1819	First visit to Venice, Italy
1828, 1833, 1840	Goes back to Italy several times
1850	Has last **exhibition** at Royal Academy
1851	Joseph dies, December 19
1897	Joseph's works displayed at what is now called the Tate Gallery in London
1987	Special gallery opens at the Tate Gallery to show Joseph's works

Glossary

abstract art that shows feelings or thoughts instead of people, places, or things as they look in real life.

ancient very old

cathedral large church

collection group of paintings or artworks

exhibit to show works of art in public

exhibition show of works of art in public

gallery room or building where works of art are shown

grounds land that surrounds a large, important house

landscape painting or drawing of the countryside

Louvre world-famous art museum in Paris, France

mast on a ship, tall pole that holds up the sail

masterpiece great work of art

oils type of paint

old master famous artist with great skill

professor person who teaches at a university or college

Royal Academy training school for artists and place where works of art are shown to the public

scene place where something happens

sketch unfinished drawing or painting

statue carved, molded, or sculptured figure

studio room or building where an artist works

style particular way an artist shows ideas in his or her work

watercolor type of paint that is thin enough to let the paper show through

---

More Books to Read

Bower, Jane. *Painting.* Danbury, Conn. Children's Press, 1998. An older reader can help you with this book.

Delafosse, Claude. *Paintings.* New York: Scholastic, Incorporated, 1996.

More Paintings to See

Fishing Boat with Hucksters Bargaining for Fish, Art Institute of Chicago, Chicago, Illinois

Conway Castle, North Wales, Getty Museum, Los Angeles, California

The Grand Canal, Venice, Metropolitan Museum of Art, New York, New York

Index